RENO air racing unlimited

Joel M Stalla,

June. 3, 1989

RENO

Air Racing Unlimited

Nigel Moll

OSPREY

Published in 1983 by Osprey Publishing Limited
12–14 Long Acre, London WC2E 9LP
Member company of the George Philip Group

British Library Cataloguing in Publication Data

Moll, Nigel
    Reno—air racing unlimited.—(Osprey
    colour series)
    I. Reno National Championship Air Races
    and Air Show
    i. Title
    629.13′074′0979355   TL506.U6R/

    ISBN 0-85045-531-6

Editor Dennis Baldry
Designed by Grub Street
Printed in Hong Kong

In a symphony of immense, furious power, seven Merlin V-12 piston engines scream at the desert floor brushing just feet beneath at 400 mph. It is a sound that courses through the spectator for the rest of his or her life. On the next 120 pages are the sights of the 1982 Reno Air Races, an outrageous annual event that has somehow survived fuel crises, a recession and the antiquity of the machines that participate. The National Air Races could happen only in America: racing a P-51 (or a P-38 or a Sea Fury or a Corsair) demands great wealth of the owners, an exceptionally cool approach of the pilots and a remote site that won't object to the din of 20,000 hp thundering overhead.

But Reno is more than the brute power of the Unlimiteds. AT-6s/SNJs (Harvards) have a class of their own: although slower than the P-51s, the AT-6s make a fine spectacle as they battle around the pylons to the rasp of transonic prop tips. In contrast to the heavyweights, the sport and racing biplanes and the IFM/Formula One racers buzz around their own, tighter course like garish insects, but still pursued by the same desire to be first that drives the heavy metal. Meshing together all this frantic speed is an air show featuring the gamut from mock battles, formation jet aerobatics, wing-walking and warbirds.
Nigel Moll
Princeton, New Jersey

Nigel Moll is Associate Editor of *Flying*, the world's most widely read aviation magazine. He works out of New York City. Formerly an editor with the British weekly, *Flight International*, Moll has a private pilot's licence and instrument rating, and flies a Beech Bonanza A36. He satisfied an old ambition by learning to fly at the age of 16, and has since flown more than 50 different types of aircraft in Europe and America.

To my wife, Chris.

The Reno races might run just once a year, but for both the racers and the fans, Unlimited air racing is a year-round passion to be advertised to all. For one week in September, as the seasons turn restless, they all head for Reno Stead Airport, tucked away inconspicuously in the desert 10 miles north of the casinos of downtown Reno. The airport is named after the brother of Nevada rancher Bill Stead. In 1964, Bill Stead revived air racing after a succession of fatal accidents in the preceding years almost snuffed out the sport

Contents

Power play

Before the racing comes the endless tuning and tweaking to extract every last horse out of the old engines that power these aging unlimiteds. Most of the Merlins slung in the P-51s are Packard-built versions of the famed Rolls-Royce V-12 that powered the Spitfire, Hurricane, Mosquito and Lancaster of WW II. The Merlins at Reno are largely specimens that have been rebuilt by a

handful of specialist engine shops, although brand-new, crated engines occasionally surface, to be quickly snapped up by teams that depend on the 1940s-vintage power to propel their racers. BELOW P-51 #81 *Habu* ground crew check out some work done in the pits. Keeping the engine uncowled for ground runs provides easier access, and improves heat dissipation

One of the more precious pieces of metal at Reno in 1982 was Lloyd Hamilton's immaculate Hawker Sea Fury, resplendent in Australian colours. Bearing the race number 16, the Sea Fury qualified at 381.467 mph by making its solo run around the course in 1:26.7. The Sea Fury is as different from a P-51 in sound as in looks: while the P-51s run tortured from gross overboost and overspeed, the Fury and its Bristol Centaurus two-row radial sigh around the pylons with a deep, rumbling whoosh. Aptly named *Baby Gorilla*, the Fury seemed most relaxed about the whole wild business of racing

For sheer brute force, the Maloney/Hinton Corsair was without equal at Reno 82: when those dormant pistons (28 of them) and spark plugs (56 of them) come alive and head for the redline, they produce a staggering 3800 hp with water injection, but without the overboost that does wonders to a Merlin's power output. Although it looks like a Goodyear F2G, the Bud Light Corsair is actually an F4U-1 modified to be similar to an F2G. The Pratt & Whitney R-4360 came out of a Douglas

C-124 Globemaster, the 13-ft, 7-in diameter prop once pulled a Douglas Skyraider, and a pair of Grumman S-2 oil coolers with drag-reducing inlets take the heat off the lubricant. Pilot-owners Steve Hinton and Jim Maloney (Hinton of *Red Baron* fame, the P-51 that brushed 500 mph with the help of a Rolls-Royce Griffon and contra-rotating prop) severed 43 in off each wing and faired off the outboard flaps in the quest for speed. The Bud Light Corsair has a considerably

hotter approach speed than a stock F2G—hotter by 15 kt—of 110 kt/130 mph. The cowling came off an A-26. The team, led by Maloney's father, Ed, who is president of the Planes of Fame at Chino, California, built the Bud Corsair in four months, using parts from various Corsair airframes. Before the races, Steve Hinton said that the airplane had been up to 450 mph in tests, using only 58 in of the 70 in of boost available. They were reluctant to boost the power over 58

because some aileron control problems had been encountered. With the original ailerons, Hinton and Maloney were experiencing some snatch at high speed, so they changed to new ailerons with a larger Friese area for more bite. Hinton and Maloney tossed a coin each day to decide who would fly the Corsair or the Bud Light II P-51

LEFT Although they didn't know it at the time, this ground crew was grooming the airplane that was to win the Unlimited class. TOP If the airplane is as clean as the pilot's flying, the winning is easier—at least, that's the theory

ABOVE Slaking *Sumthin' Else's* thirst

OVERLEAF P-51 #69, *Jeannie*, was the hard-luck story of Reno 82. She blew two engines and never qualified

Poor *Jeannie*! She won in 1980 and 1981, and she dates back to 1946, when she raced in the Thompson Trophy as #77, *Galloping Ghost*. *Jeannie*, alias N79111, has one of the most colourful histories of all the Unlimiteds now flying. As *Galloping Ghost* she took fourth place in the 1946 Thompson, flown by B. Raymond; she took the same place in the 1949 Sohio Trophy, piloted by S. Beville. She flew as the *Galloping Ghost*

throughout the 1960s, but was not raced. From 1969 to 1979 she flew and raced as #69, *Miss Candace*, before being renamed *Jeannie* after the wife of the current owner, Wiley Sanders. *Jeannie*'s string of successes snapped in 1982: the pits talk before qualifying centred on #69 *Jeannie*, #4 *Dago Red*, John Crocker's #6 *Sumthin' Else* and the Bud Light Corsair #1. Would *Jeannie* make it a hat-trick and take first

place again? It looked doubtful when she threw a con rod during pre-qualifying practice. But after a 15-hour engine change—with the help and floodlights of a competing crew (Tired Iron of P-51 #81 *Habu*)—that extended well past midnight, *Jeannie* was in with a chance again. Until, that is, she blew a second engine while trying to qualify the next day. The prop governor let go, and *Jeannie* howled like a hyena as pilot Skip Holm

converted speed into altitude. Reno old-timers feared the prop would throw a blade, so loud was the howl; but Holm, with an oil-covered windshield, made a superb deadstick touchdown that kept *Jeannie* free of further damage. The pits erupted in a cheer for Holm's performance, but she was not to race at Reno 82

ABOVE Blown engine? Never fear, Mike is here.
Mike Wilton brought this Packard-built V-1650-
9A in the back of a Chevy van for precisely the
eventuality shown on the preceding pages and to
the right. The price was $40,000 'this week only.'
This particular Merlin powered *Red Baron* before
being replaced by a Rolls-Royce Griffon. Wilton
helped rebuild the engine to its current condition,
a task that took about 600 hours. Said Wilton:
'We think it's running at 2000 to 2500 hp, but it's
hard to tell because we can't find a dynamometer
big enough.' Sitting in the back of the Chevy, the
engine weighed some 1800 lb; each piston, without
con rod or pin, weighs $3\frac{1}{4}$ lb. Redline for such an

engine stands at 3500 rpm, at which the 10-in diameter supercharger impeller is spinning at 30,000 rpm. ABOVE John Crocker's luck ran out in the Unlimited Gold final when his P-51, #6 *Sumthin' Else*, pulled out after three good laps. The Merlin was turning at 3750 rpm, and ran out of induction cooling. With the induction temperature at 100°, the engine detonated once, snapping the crankshaft in half. The engine then tore its own innards apart. With oil covering the cowling and windshield, Crocker made a blind landing under the guidance of pace pilot Bob Hoover circling overhead in the yellow Rockwell International P-51. Crocker, a World Airways

DC-10 check captain, won at Reno in 1979. Since buying *Sumthin' Else* in 1976, he had spent between $300,000 and $350,000 on the airplane. *Sumthin' Else*'s engine, when running on 145-octane avgas, turns out somewhere between 3200 and 3400 hp, according to Crocker. The most powerful Merlins at Reno turn out almost double their military horsepower, so the occasional mechanical failure is inevitable. Crocker did some fine flying after losing his engine, but, with no forward vision and only verbal guidance from above, he hit his propeller on the runway while landing. The results are shown on page 24

ABOVE The four Corsairs made for good variety around the pylons. This one, #82 *Wart Hog*, was flown by Mike Wright, from Casper, Wyoming. It qualified at 304.038 mph, compared with 333.433 mph and 346.861 mph by the two other F4Us at Reno 82, flown, respectively, by Bob Guilford and Robert Yancey

RIGHT *Fat Cat*, Clay Klabo's P-51 #85, qualified at 410.847 mph and was placed second in the Unlimited Gold final, at 386.482 mph and 11:24.8

OVERLEAF #72 *Mangia Pane*'s Merlin with the wraps off

RIGHT Other AT-6 crews lent manpower and tools to get Philip Gist's airplane back in the air after a collapsed gear leg damaged the left wing on landing. Here, Gary Williams and Red Mayer try to coax some more life out of a hydraulic gear actuator for Gist's AT-6, #49 *Whipper Snapper*. The wingtip and aileron linkages needed some work, but the effort paid off: Gist flew *Whipper Snapper* into fifth place in the AT-6/SNJ Silver race at a speed of 206.446 mph. Gist's brother Jimmy was also racing at Reno, in #68 *Texas Red*

ABOVE The risk to man and machine is ever present, waiting to pounce on the smallest mistake or mechanical malfunction. After John Crocker's burst engine covered his windshield with oil, he was forced to land virtually blind. His skill kept the airplane in one piece, but the prop became a casualty when it struck the runway on landing. Good sportsmanship and a strong spirit of camaraderie are always evident at Reno. Crocker, who was putting on a strong performance in the Gold until his engine quit, was among the first to shake the hand of the winner, Ron Hevle in #4 *Dago Red*

ABOVE Piston engines don't come any bigger than this Pratt & Whitney R-4360, the powerplant for the Hinton/Maloney Super Corsair. It has 28 cylinders, 28 pistons and 56 spark plugs in its four-row radial configuration. The 4360 stands for cubic inches' displacement: to put that figure in perspective, its cubic capacity is 71 litres or, put another way, 42 Volkswagen Rabbit/Golf engines. The 4360 in the Hinton and Maloney/Bud Light Corsair put out about 4000 hp, twice the power available to WW2 Corsairs. According to pilot Jim Maloney, the airplane burns fuel at a rate of 400 gallons per hour at race speed and low altitude. The water-injection system runs at 100 gallons per hour. Just as the Bud Corsair is a highly modified

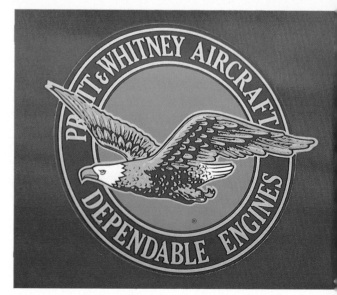

F4U, so was the original Vought-Goodyear F2G a similar adaptation of the F4U, produced in response to a US Navy requirement for a more powerful Corsair. Only 10 F2Gs were built, however, because the cessation of WW2 brought production to an end. Although Hinton and Maloney's Corsair is registered as a Vought-Goodyear F2G, it is considerably modified from wartime factory standard. Computer projections indicate that the airplane should be capable of 480 mph and, with a bit more tweaking, 500 mph. At Reno 82, the airplane's first outing, it was far below 480 but still put on a fine performance for a first race. Steve Hinton qualified the airplane at 413.208 mph, and in the Unlimited Gold final he came in fourth at 362.496. With the bugs worked out, this airplane promises to be a formidable contender at future Reno races. Two Hawker Sea Furies, however, are destined to receive R-4360 transplants, which should make for some exciting jockeying around Reno's pylons in the years ahead

RIGHT It is inevitable that the Unlimiteds draw the most attention and crowds at Reno, but the IFM/Formula Ones and Racing Biplanes are actually purer racers, designed solely for the purpose of being first over the finishing line. Here, Dusty Dowd, from Syracuse, Kansas, takes a close look at the Continental O-200 of #5 *Illusion*, a Cassutt. Until 1968, the midgets had all been powered by 190-in^3 Continentals, 85-hp flat-fours. Goodyear Tire and Rubber sponsored the first race for these formula airplanes in 1947 at Cleveland. It was this class of racer that kept the sport alive after 1949, the year that a P-51 crashed at Cleveland with the loss of innocent lives. In that accident, Bill Odom crashed while rounding a pylon. The airplane collided with a house, killing a mother and child, and in the process helped put an end to heavy-metal racing for 15 years until its revival at Reno in 1964

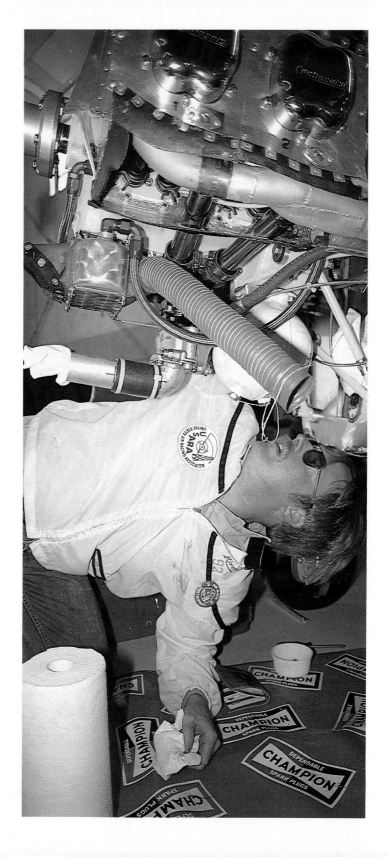

ABOVE If it hadn't been for Don Beck's *Sorceress*, there probably would be no Racing Biplane class. When *Sorceress* appeared in 1968, she met all the formula criteria for the Sport Biplane class but was 50 mph faster than the other contenders—aircraft such as the Pitts Special, Mong Sport and Starduster. For five years, the Sport Biplane pilots had to be content with second place to *Sorceress* and Don Beck, but in 1973 *Sundancer*, developed by Sid White from the homebuilt Midget Mustang, appeared and toppled Beck. These two 'super biplanes' dominated the field, and the other pilots cried foul. In 1980 another challenger entered the fray, *Cobra*. All three were at Reno 82: Don Beck and *Sorceress*, Pat Hines with *Sundancer* and Al Kramer with *Cobra*, along with two others—Dan Mortensen in the Amsoil/Rutan tandem-wing special and Tom Aberle in #25 *Two Bits*. All five raced in their own Racing Division of the Biplane Class, and their speeds ranged from 202 to 223 mph in qualifying, with Pat Hines in *Sundancer* fastest. Hines also took the Gold final, at 209.401 mph, closely followed by Mortensen at 209.206 and Beck at 206.289. Kramer pulled *Cobra* out of the race in the sixth and final lap after being lapped by the leaders

ABOVE *Pony Express* was a brave homebuilt assault
on the Unlimiteds, but it was not fast enough to
qualify. Using 80-percent power from *Pony*'s
Lycoming TIO-540, pilot Hal Goddard reached
265 mph—not enough to place him among the
Unlimiteds. He said after his attempt at qualifying
that he could probably have reached 300 if he'd
gunned the engine more, 'but I didn't come here
to blow an engine!' *Pony Express*, racing as #3, is
a Raiderhawk 1 and was built specifically to race.
The engine is basically a 310-hp Navajo
powerplant, with a Chieftain propeller, but has
been boosted to more than 400 hp. Water-alcohol
cooling keeps the turbo outlet temperature down

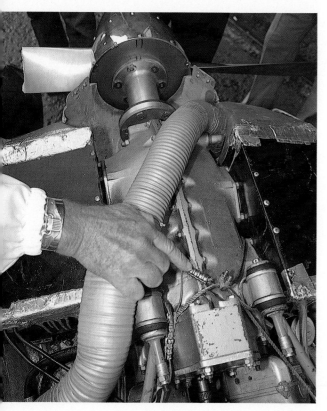

FAR LEFT Bill Chatburn, a trustee on the Air Race Committee, was nearly in the doghouse. Executive Director General Floyd Edsall has directed the races since 1980, assisted by 24 trustees

ABOVE AND LEFT Rocky Jones had just got the green flag to start his qualifying run in Formula One/IFM #97 *Ol' Blu* when he heard a loud bang. The airplane had been running well at 3500 rpm and 230 mph, said Jones, when the propeller shed most of one blade. Having stretched his glide, he ran out of speed and dived at the runway to regain some. He said that he hit the runway level, but still with a high rate of descent. It was a 10G impact, violent enough to splay and break both landing-gear legs. The propeller imbalance had created enough vibration to shake the engine clean off its primary mounts, and the backup cable restraint saved the day for Jones. He had a prop break at Reno 81, too, and he thinks the powerplant has a resonance problem, a theory born out by a crack on the other blade

31

Unlimiteds

ABOVE Bob Hoover probably has more time in Mustangs than all the Unlimited pilots combined. He flew them in combat in WW2, and he has since become a permanent fixture at the air races. It's Hoover who proclaims the famous line, 'Gentlemen, you have a race,' as the Unlimiteds thunder down the chute that leads them into the pylon course. He then pulls up into a steep climb and circles overhead the course listening for a Mayday

Without the spectators and their support, there would be no Reno National Air Races. In 1982, the 82,000-strong crowd was treated to snow, thunderstorms, biting cold and desert heat—all in the space of a week. But their enthusiasm was never dampened. The last three days of race week are the public days, with Gold Sunday pulling the most fans. Throughout the week, all the activity is in the pits, but on Gold Sunday, the Unlimiteds line up before the grandstands like shining warriors. A strong pair of binoculars and a super-telephoto camera lens are essential, though, because the Unlimited course extends about three miles north into the desert around nine pylons. The entire course measures 9.187 miles over the ground. An airplane averaging 350 mph completes one lap in 94.5 seconds, or 82.69 seconds at 400 mph, or 73.5 seconds at 450 mph. Armed with information like this in the race program, the spectators can get involved in the races' progress despite their remoteness from the outfield pylons. The crowd gets the best view as the Unlimiteds streak past the home-pylon start/finish line, right in front of the grandstands. And at Pylon One, level with the east end of the crowd, the racers turn steeply as they head northeast into the desert for Two, Three and the long straight to Four

Dago Red made history at Reno 82 by winning on its first outing. The airplane flew only three weeks before race week, making its victory all the more impressive. Owners Frank Taylor and Bill 'Tiger' Destefani spent, between them, about $500,000 to get *Dago Red* ready for racing. According to pilot Ron Hevle, the plan was to blow one engine in qualifying and set a new record, and to race with a second engine. But there wasn't time. Hevle kept *Dago Red*'s race boost and reduction-gear ratio a secret, but one pit crewmember foresaw the engine turning at up to 4000 rpm. He also revealed some of the measures that would help boost *Dago Red*'s power to almost double the normal 1800 hp for take-off and 1600 max continuous. The fuel started as 140-octane, but then received shots of liquid manganese (a flame-retardent anti-detonation agent). Further down the induction system were introduced ADI (Alcohol Distilled-water Injection, to increase the density of the induction air) and nitrous oxide (which boosts power by some 200 hp because it adds oxygen to the combustion process). The *Dago Red* team, according to this pit crewmember, has access to 18 Rolls-Royce Griffons, and intends to break the *Red Baron* Griffon Mustang's 499.018 mph record by 30 mph

ABOVE *Dago Red* in full, furious flight around
Pylon Seven in the Unlimited Gold final, with
victory just seconds away

RIGHT Its R-4360 silent at day's end, the
Hinton/Maloney Corsair enjoys a brief period free
of technicians, torque wrenches and tweaking

Few pilots nowadays get to sit behind a snout like the Super Corsair's. Jim Maloney and Steve Hinton tossed a coin for the privilege each day. Despite the antiquity of the airframe and engine, the instrument panel is every inch up to date

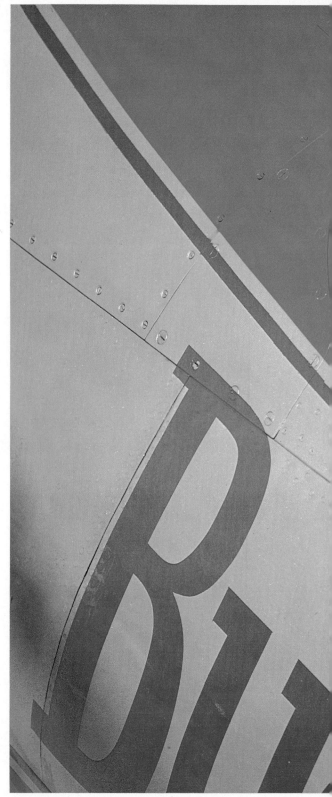

The Maloney/Hinton Corsair brought back memories of the late 1940s' National Air Races for those old enough to recall Cook Cleland, Tony Janazzo, Ron Puckett and Ben McKillen, who flew the monsters in 1947, 1948 and 1949. Janazzo perished in his F2G-1 in the 1947 Thompson when he flew into the ground at about 400 mph. Cleland, however, flew his F2G-1 to victory in the same race at 396 mph. The R-4360-powered Corsairs were banned from the 1948 Tinnerman Trophy, because they were deemed to have an unfair advantage over the rest of the field. But in 1949 they were back: Ben McKillen flew an F2G-1 to victory at 386 mph. The first three places in the 1949 Thompson also fell to F2Gs, but that was the last year of the Unlimiteds until their revival by Bill Stead at Reno in 1964

LEFT Jim Maloney flew the Bud Light Mustang #0, stablemate of the Bud Light Corsair. He qualified at 362.446 mph and placed seventh at 334.834 in the Silver final

ABOVE Howard Pardue brought his Wildcat to Reno primarily to participate in the air show, not really expecting to be fast enough to race. But he did qualify (second slowest, at 325.044 mph) and, thanks to some no-shows and the failure of *Jeannie* to qualify, he was able to enter the field in the 21st and final position. (FG1D *Wart Hog*, the Tired Iron Racing Team's Corsair, took the 22nd position as alternate, but did get to race.) Pardue flew the old 'cat into last place in the Unlimited Bronze final, picking up $2067 in the process

OVERLEAF P-51 #86 *No Name Lady* was the mount of rookie Delbert Williams. Having qualified eighth fastest, at 396.609 mph, Williams took the lead in the fifth lap of the first Silver heat and held it to the chequered flag. It was the first Unlimited race he had ever flown. Williams's consistently strong performance in the heats put him in the Gold final, in which he again flew a fine race, placing third behind *Dago Red* and *Fat Cat*. Williams grew up and went to school with the owner of #86, Joe Banducci. Banducci took the airplane out of racing in 1980, but he and Williams got talking and decided to race. Bob Love, a veteran of the pylons, checked Williams out on the finer points of hurtling around at ground level with six other warbirds

45

ABOVE AND OVERLEAF Lefty Gardner and his P-38 are a familiar sight at Reno. His racing around the pylons is consistently among the most spectacular of the flying, although, with its superchargers removed, the airplane is not particularly fast. It qualified at 345.376 mph, and Gardner flew it into third place in the Bronze final, at 335.201 mph. He seems to have a peculiarly accurate feel for his wingspan, and places the tip low, very low, in turns

RIGHT Rookie Delbert Williams banks #86 *No Name Lady* high around Pylon Seven on his way to third place in the Gold final

ABOVE Lefty Gardner and P-38 #13 in full fury, heading for third place in the Bronze final

RIGHT Despite *Jeannie*'s untimely departure from the field, Skip Holm got to race by flying #68 *Shangri-La*, the only airworthy P-51B. Bob Love, rather than compete in his own Mustang, *Illegitimatus Non Carborundum*, flew #2, a P-51D owned by engine man Jack Hovey. The engine in #2 is a Merlin 622 out of a Canadair North Star

and Hovey, by limiting race boost to stock power (1720 hp), hopes to see a TBO (time between overhaul) of 1400 hours. He likes to race his airplane not to win, but just for the fun of it

OVERLEAF Lloyd Hamilton's immaculate Hawker Sea Fury, #16 *Baby Gorilla*, glowing in the desert dusk

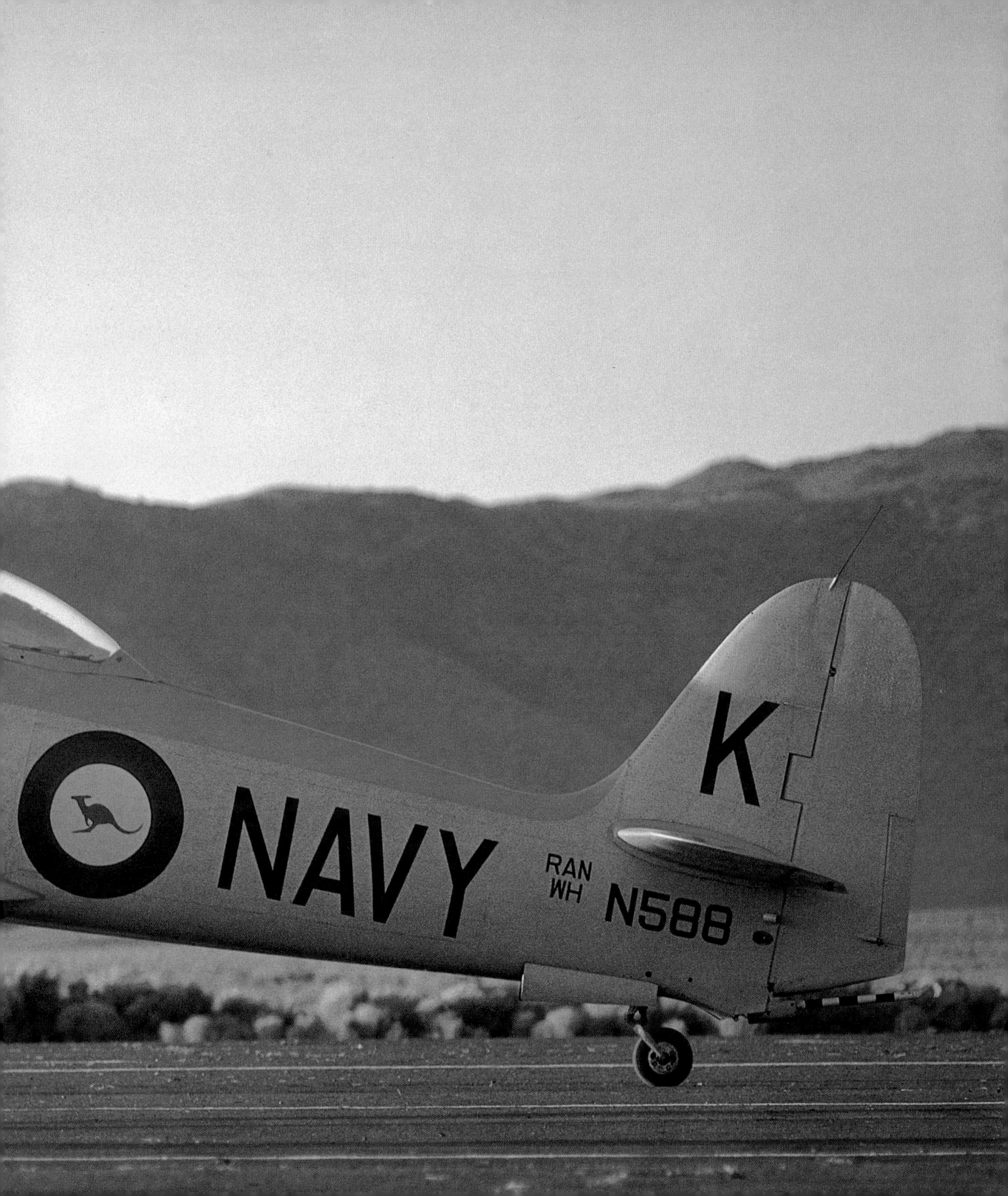
K
NAVY
RAN
WH
N588

The Sea Fury represented the end of an era for the British Royal Navy. It was the last (and to many the most beautiful) piston-engine fighter to serve with the Fleet Air Arm. The airplane packs a 2480-hp Bristol Cenaurus with 18 cylinders. With a wing area of just 280 ft^2 and a gross weight of 12,500 lb, the Sea Fury has a top speed of 460 mph at 18,000 ft. Lloyd Hamilton's Sea Fury is painted in Royal Australian Navy colors and has the standard Centaurus, but a pair of Sea Furies should be flying soon with Pratt & Whitney R-4360s—the corncob radial of the F2G

The Maloney/Hinton P-51, #o *Bud Light II*, flew
in the shadow of the R-4360 Corsair's limelight

LEFT Clay Klabo in #85 *Fat Cat* streaks toward the chequered flag, second place and $16,374 in the Gold final.

OVERLEAF F4U-4 #101, owned and flown by Bob Yancey, has a DC-7 spinner around the hub of its big four-blade propeller for a whisker more speed and better cooling

Although an old Corsair is hardly suited to instrument flying, there's no harm in having a full complement of new instruments and avionics to keep track of Old Hose Nose's progress, pulse and position. This one is #82 *Wart Hog*, flown by Mike Wright of the Casper, Wyoming, Tired Iron Racing Team

ABOVE P-51B #68 *Shangri-La* sips on a volatile cocktail: Avgas 115–145, a brew that is now as rare as the antiques that consume it. A suitable quantity is shipped into Reno each year to quench the thirst of the Unlimiteds and any other visiting relics

LEFT Crinkled Corsair canvas

OVERLEAF P-51 #19 *Lou IV*, flown by John Dilley and owned by Tom Kelley, qualified at 403.037 mph and placed sixth in the Gold final

LEFT Jim Orton, flying John Sandberg's #28
Tipsy Too, passed Bob Love in the Hovey
Mustang just short of the home pylon and went
on to win the Saturday Silver heat at 362.903
mph. Love finished in fourth place, just a shade
slower at 360.098. There was less than one second
between the chequered-flag times of Skip/Holm
(*Shangri-La*, second), Mike Wright (*Habu*, third)
and Love

ABOVE Jim Orton and Bob Love battled again in
the Silver final. Orton beat Love to the flag, but
when the judges had had their say, the two pilots'
positions were reversed: Love fourth and Orton,
who cut Pylon Three on the pace lap, fifth

Although #81 *Habu* was flown primarily by Earl Ketchen of Tired Iron, team-mate Mike Wright stepped into the airplane for Saturday's Silver heat as Ketchen was feeling under the weather. On Sunday, though, Ketchen was back on form: he flew *Habu* to victory in the Silver final, collecting $4950

OVERLEAF Skip Holm, Bob Love and Jim Orton jockey for the advantage between Pylons Six and Seven in Friday's Silver heat. The three pilots finished in that order, each separated by half a second at the flag

TIRED IRON
RACING TEAM

TEAM MEMBERS
•DON DAVIS•JACK SUTTLE
•MIKE WRIGHT•PAUL KETCHEN
•JACK MUCK•CHUCK REESE
•RUSS JOHNSON

ABOVE Bob Love in the Hovey Mustang #2

LEFT Delbert Williams and #86 *No Name Lady*.

RIGHT *Ridge Runner*, flown by Dan Martin, was the only Unlimited airframe serious casualty at Reno 82. The airplane was severely damaged in an off-airport forced landing. The Merlin threw a con rod out of the side of its casing, and a ruptured fuel line started a fire with which Martin became preoccupied. 'I'm on fire,' he repeated over his radio. Unfortunately for Martin, he was unable to make the runway and attempted to land on a dirt track with the wheels down. *Ridge Runner* clipped a wing in the dirt and sustained heavy damage, but Martin was unscathed

LEFT George Roberts (who always flies with no socks) taxies out for a late-evening ride in Wiley Sanders' #96, *Jeannie*'s stablemate. #96 was the first Mustang built in Australia, hence the art on the left main gear door. Roberts won the Bronze final and, at the subsequent awards banquet, he put his trophy to fine use by filling it with champagne. He brought some glory to the ill-fated *Jeannie* team

ABOVE Bill 'Tiger' Destefani in #72 *Mangia Pane* finished second in the Gold final behind *Dago Red*. He owns both airplanes. But the judges ordained that he had cut Pylon One on lap two and Pylon Eight on lap five, and Destefani incurred a 64-second time penalty, pushing him back to fifth place

Air show

No air show would be complete without jet aerobatics. Enter the Canadian Armed Forces Snowbirds, who have flown at Reno for six years in a row. The team's nine Canadair Tutors are relatively slow and low-powered, but thosse qualities are no handicap when combined with Snowbird choreography. The team performed 23 different manoeuvers for its 1982 routine, including five-abreast loops and rolls. And plenty of smoke

LEFT The Eagles team up briefly with the two Pitts S-2As of the Ray-Ban Reds (Rod Ellis and Bill Cowan), Canada's only civilian aerobatic team

ABOVE The Eagles, in person, are Tom Poberezny (left), Gene Soucy (centre) and leader Charlie Hillard. Their airplanes are 260-hp Christen Eagles, perfectly suited to the task. Charlie Hillard is a businessman with an automobile sales organization. He is a former World Aerobatic Champion, and has 23 years' experience in aerobatics. Tom Poberezny, equally well known for his untiring efforts at the Experimental Aircraft Association, flies right wing. Gene Soucy was reared on aerobatics; his job puts him in the right seat of a regional-airline DC-9

OVERLEAF The Confederate Air Force B-17 Flying Fortress brought some old grace to the races

83

Bob Bishop flies the world's smallest jet at air shows across the nation. He does not call the airplane a BD-5J, but rather an Acrojet, since it is modified from BD standard. The Acrojet is 100 lb lighter than a BD, and it has tankage for just 36 gallons of fuel in the wings, giving one hour, 20 minutes' endurance. Bishop's airplane also stalls about 13 kt slower. Its TRS-18 turbojet has a one-stage compressor and a one-stage turbine, and produces 200 lb of thrust at 44,000 rpm; the turbine has a diameter of only 6 in. Fuel metering is controlled by a computer. Bob Bishop is the pilot who had the famous mishap in a BD-5J. He was flying at the 250-kt redline when the canopy unlatched, swung back and hit him on the head, lifting Bishop out of his seat momentarily. The shock made Bishop pull back on the stick, pegging the airplane's G meter at 10.5G; the load was later calculated to be 14.5G. Not quite expecting such loads, the left wing bent upwards by 23°, and the right wing by 19°. Blinded by blood, Bishop had to rely on Corky Fornoff (also in a BD-5J and with whom Bishop had been flying) for guidance back to the runway. The BD-5J's ultimate load factor was thought to be 9G, but it held together and took Bishop back to the ground. It was the only day he had flown the little jet without a parachute. Because of its diminutive airframe, the Acrojet seems to be much higher and faster than it actually is during Bishop's routine. He reaches 2000 ft at the top of a loop, but his altitude looks more like 5000 ft when viewed from the ground. In a tailslide he peaks at 2300 ft, and the highest speed Bishop reaches in a display is 230 kt

RIGHT Bob Bishop enjoys a cool Coors after the day's flying is done. It was perhaps prophetic that he should have chosen Coors as his brew at Reno 82. Bishop is now sponsored by the brewery, and his Acrojet is known as the Coors *Silver Bullet*

Bob Hoover taught himself aerobatics at the age of 16. Since then, he has become probably the most watched pilot in history. He has attended all 19 Reno Air Races in his dual role as Unlimited starter pilot and air-show performer. Hoover and the yellow Rockwell International Mustang are inseparable, and his aerobatic routine in a stock Shrike Commander has become one of the most famous acts in aviation history. As can be seen, left, the word 'low' needs redefining when Hoover flies the Shrike. Much of his display in the general-aviation twin is made with both engines shut down, including the falling-leaf approach and landing. Hoover's precision is quite uncanny: he lands, powerless, and manages the Shrike's momentum so perfectly that he barely needs to touch the brakes as he pulls up, nose first, directly in front of the grandstand

AT-6/SNJ class

After a two-year hiatus, the AT-6s/SNJs returned to Reno in 1981 with their own special racing course. It was in 1978 that two airplanes collided while racing on the small Formula One circuit, with the loss of two pilots' lives. From 1981 on, the old trainers got their own five-mile circuit; in 1978 they had used the Formulas' 3.108-mile course. The larger course, while still making for an exciting race, gave the airplanes plenty of space

Four AT-6s/SNJs rumble down the chute for the start of the Silver final. Nearest is Alfred Goss in #75, who won the event at 215.569 mph. #77 *Wildcatter*, flown by Tired Iron pilot Mike Wright (also of P-51 *Habu* and Corsair *Wart Hog*), came in third at 209.497 mph. Wearing bad-guys paint, #11 was flown into fourth place by Ray Schutte. And Jim Fox, in #72 *Terrible Texan*, took sixth place at 204.569 mph

Ralph Twombly cleaned up in the AT-6/SNJ class. He qualified fastest, at 219.245 mph, and went on to win the Gold final at 214.900 mph. The Gold final carried a $20,000 purse, $4500 of which went to Twombly when he took the chequered flag. His steed was #44 *Miss Behavin'*, which has a long racing history

1981 NATIONAL CLASS CHAMPION

MIAMI, FLA. 1973
MOJAVE, CALIF. 1975
FT. LAUDERDALE 1970
ST. LOUIS, MO. 1969
CAPE MAY, N.J. 1971
WILSON, N.C. 1971
RENO CHAMPIONSHIPS
71 72 76 77 78
81 82

Crew Chief
E.E. Doctor MAPLES

SKY PRINTS

AVIATION

Texas Red, flown by Jimmy Gist, from Grapevine, Texas

LEFT Jim Fox, heading for sixth place in the Silver final aboard #72 *Terrible Texan*

BELOW Jerry McDonald was the fourth fastest qualifier in #5 *Big Red*. He took seventh and last position in the Gold final, at 204.983 mph

OVERLEAF #8 *Phoenix*, better known at Reno 82 as *Rent A Dent*, was flown by Bob Jones into second place in the Silver final. His speed was 210.354 mph

Alfred Goss takes a pylon in #75 *Warlock*, a
particularly well restored airplane

IFM/Formula 1/Sport and Racing Biplanes

With their own special class, the Racing Biplanes were set apart from the stock Sport Biplanes, making for fairer racing and some close battles at the pylons. *Sundancer*'s Midget Mustang heritage can be seen, ABOVE, as the airplane hitches a tail-first ride across the ramp in preparation for a race-horse start onto the course

Firmly in the Rutan mould, the Amsoil/Rutan
Special qualified second fastest, at 212.327 mph,
flown by Dan Mortensen of Superior, Wisconsin.
Mortensen finished second in the Gold final, just
0.2 mph and 0.3 seconds behind winner Pat Hines
in *Sundancer*

PYLON RACER
38
The Flying Dutchman

OWNED BY...*TOM ASLETT & BURTON WEBB* TWIN FALLS, ID.
PILOTED BY...*TOM ASLETT*
BUILT BY *ELDON LUTZ*

Small enough to be disassembled and trucked to
Reno, the IFM/Formula Ones are pure racers,
designed solely to extract every last knot from the
formula. Tom Aslett, flying #38 *Flying
Dutchman*, placed third in the Silver final

Dennis Brown hitched a video camera onto the fin
of Pitts Special #29 *Scarlet*, which he qualified at
147.958 mph and flew into sixth place in the Gold
final at 143.171. The Gold final was flown in some
of the worst conditions thrown at Reno 82,
through rain and dim visibility

Stan Brown's #2 *Washoe Zephyr II*, another
Pitts, did not race. Brown raced his other Pitts,
#00 *Tonopah Low*, instead, qualifying at 171.455
mph and taking fourth place in the Gold final at
165.458

OVERLEAF Earl Allen's Pitts S-1 #42 *Flat Wing*

LEFT IFM/Formula One #2, a WAR-101, flown by Bob Drew into first place in the Silver final at 205.252 mph

ABOVE Jim Miller, in # *Texas Gem*, was one of the four unfortunates in the Gold final whose time was not taken by the pylon judges. In fact, the timing of the first three finishers was later questioned by racing participants. *Texas Gem* is unique among the IFM/Formula field by virtue of its small four-blade pusher propeller and tail configuration

Deke Slayton, the astronaut, brought #21 *Stinger* to Reno. He qualified at 213.664 mph, but failed to start in the Silver final, which was flown in cold drizzle and poor visibility. Canopies fogged, and carburetors were prone to icing

Don Beck took a break from flying *Sorceress*, the wicked racing biplane, to race #18 into second place in the Silver final, at 203.823 mph

Up close and personal

For Ron Hevle, Bill Destefani, Frank Taylor and
the entire *Dago Red* team, Reno 82 was a dream
come true. At Reno 81, the airplane was little
more than an idea, but one year later it was the
Unlimited champion at its first races

An exuberant crew rides *Dago Red* back to the pits. Apart from the satisfaction of victory, Ron Hevle (right) received the coveted trophy and a check for $26,608. His winning speed in the Gold final was 405.092. It would have been higher if John Crocker in #6 *Sumthin' Else* had continued to hound him around the pylons. But after Crocker dropped out with a blown engine, Hevle throttled back and loafed across the finish line. There was simply no point in taking the Merlin to its limits when the race was virtually in the bag

No expense was spared in getting *Dago Red* to
Reno in style. The crew had their own *Dago*
barbecue and there was even a bottle of *Dago*
wine on hand for Hevle when he landed. The
team truck was suitably flamboyant, too

UHALT'S
BAR-B-Q PITS
BAKERSFIELD, CA.

LEFT Wiley Sanders' second P-51, #96, was hijacked briefly by a skinny pink cat that shied away from Clay Klabo's *Fat Cat*

ABOVE Air combat, Australian style, as depicted on #96 gear door

LEFT Fat Cat, Formula One variety, poses proudly as Norton Thomas makes a few adjustments deep within #11 *Hell's Angel*

RIGHT Jimmy Gist's *Texas Red*, one of the more colorful AT-6s racing

OVERLEAF Despite her run of bad luck at Reno 82, *Jeannie* is still the most accomplished Unlimited

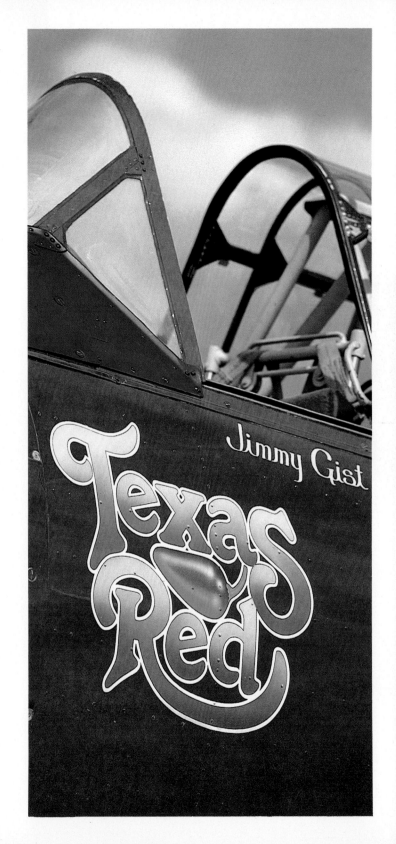